THE SECRET RECORD OF ME

WHITECAP BOOKS
Vancouver • Toronto

First published in Australia in 1997 by Roland Harvey Books

Copyright © Roland Harvey 1997

First published in Canada by Whitecap Books
351 Lynn Avenue
North Vancouver
British Canada
V7J 2C4
Phone (604) 9809852 Fax (604) 9808197
Whitecap Books Toronto
Phone (416) 4443442 Fax (416) 4446630

ISBN 1 55285 100 1

Printed in China at Everbest Printing Co Ltd.

THE SECRET RECORD OF ME

by Me
and Roland Harvey

we are the turkeys of good luck and long life.

the SECRET RECORD of me INTRO

This is my BOOK to fill in, write in, draw in, stick in, keep in AND HIDE in. I keep it until I am VERY OLD. I can look in it every BIRTHDAY. I can record my autographs, Tickets, Hair, PHOTOS, BEST things, WORST things, things I am GOOD at and things I am trying to IMPROVE. I can remember my ADVENTURES, my HOME, my SCHOOL, my Hobbies and interests. I can collect things that happen...

This book is all about ME and my FRIENDS, my Family and the NEW things my Holidays, and the... I can predict what Life Has

START →

ON ON

CUTTINGS

GIRL SAVES WORLD

secrets

and

INTERESTINGNESS LEVEL ▶

I am the serpent of everything else

PERSONAL DETAILS

SECRET
IDENTITY
CARD
AGENT 999.9

LIFT FLAP ↓

STICK PHOTO HERE

and I live at

My name

I LIVE HERE

PRESS

date I was born crawled
First burp First word ran..
went to school moved house...
First pet First bike accidents trips
and anything else interesting!

TiMeline

MY AGE THIS

hands

third finger

first finger

little finger

second finger

thumb

Fingerprints

Put your left hand **Here** and draw around it.

↓ To my left elbow ↓

PRESS!

THIS
is a drawing
OF YOUR BELLY
BUTTON. FINISH
The Drawing.

SIGNED . . . .

FAMILY PHOTOS

These are my relatives. Paste pictures of yours on this page. I bet mine are prettier.

...the furthest place from me...

...the worst place...

places I'd like to go...

The author of the book I'm reading lives...

Another use for Chopsticks

...where my pen friend lives...

...where my pet comes from...

...the route my ancestors took to come here...

...and anything else at all!

THIS IS A DRAWING OF
MY HOME

MOON
(NO MAIL
SERVICE)

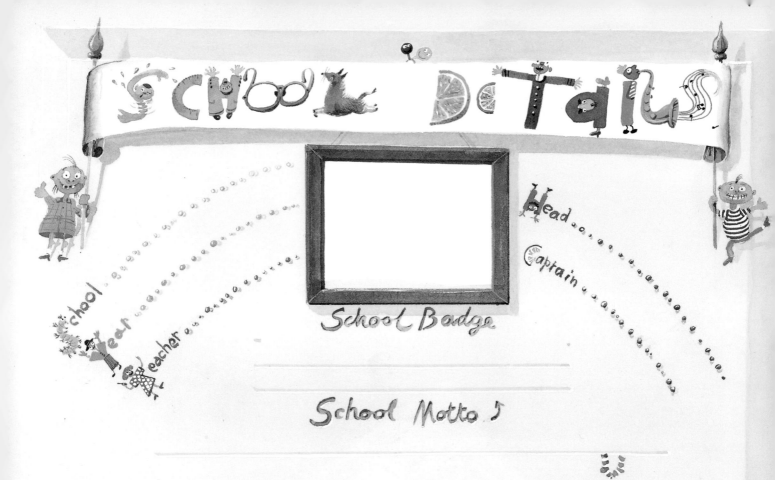

SCHOOL DETAILS

School Badge

School

Teacher

Head

Captain

_____

School Motto

_____

Teams and Clubs

School Photos

▼

Tallest kid..................................

Quietest kid.........

Friendliest kid.......

Funniest kid...............

Youngest kid...........

Fastest kid.............

HOBBIES

swapping   collecting   making   cooking   creating   watching

drawing   reading   playing   writing   finding   doing   breeding

& INTERESTS

THINGS I WOULD LIKE TO TRY

COLLECTIONS

Pop collection

collection di pasta

collection

stamp and...

knife

shoe collection

coin collection

collection

pet collection

pip collection

yellow sock collection

Tie Collection

my sticker collection

Autograph Book

STAMPS

HERE & THERE

Nose Print

Lip Print

Doctor's Warning: If your lips won't fit in this space, see doctor immediately (or a vet).

FLASHBACKS

Good Things I've Seen

Things I Remember...

Things I Can't Quite Remember...

Great Smells

Cool Sounds

Emergency Vent For Bad Memories

Great Tastes

Strange Feelings

Great Meals

SAVINGS

BIRTHDAYS TO SAVE FOR

Name	Date	$

holidays   clothes

christmas   gifts

travel   sports

concerts

jewelry

books

magazines

C.D. Roms

emergencies

films

hobbies   pets

tickets

treats

fish and chips

C.D.s

adventures

games

Music things to save for

SECRET THINGS I'M SAVING FOR

sport things to save for

WISHES

people I'd like to meet...

things I'd like to have...

secret wishes

groups I'd like to see...

books I'd like to read...

most important wishes...

Things I'd like

to hear... ?

Things I'd like to do...

ADVENTURES

I WOULD

LIKE TO HAVE ONE DAY

YOUNG OLD INTERESTING FAMOUS ADVENTUROUS KIND THOUGHTFUL HUGE

... AND PEOPLE I'VE MET

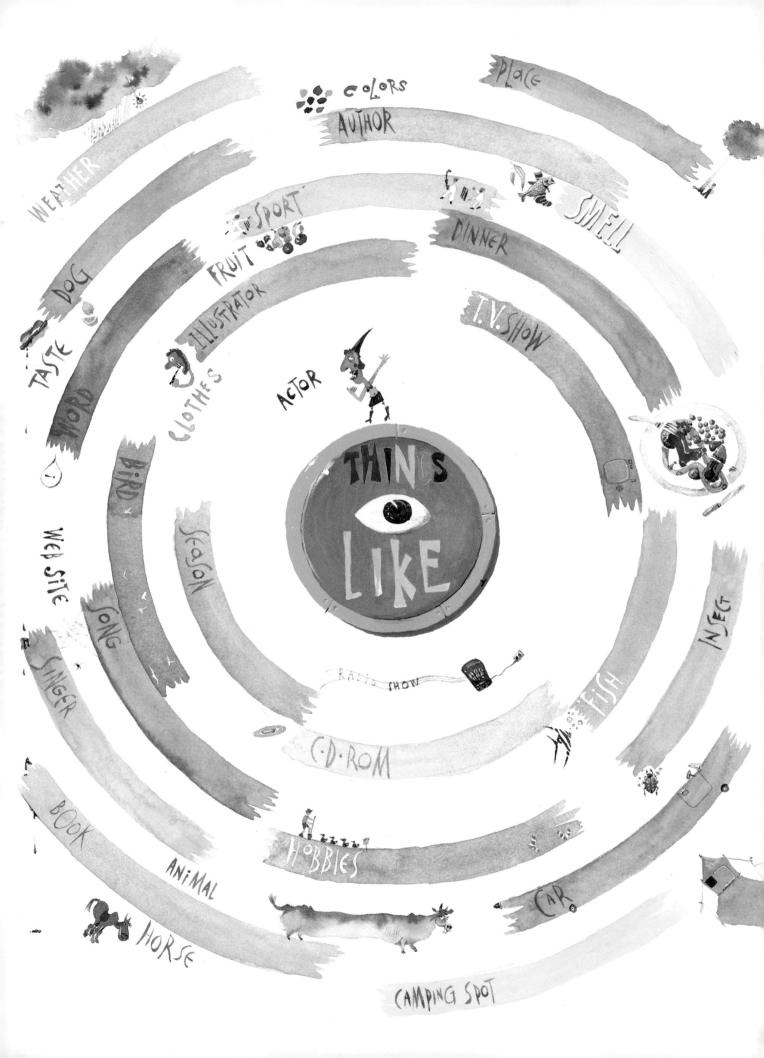

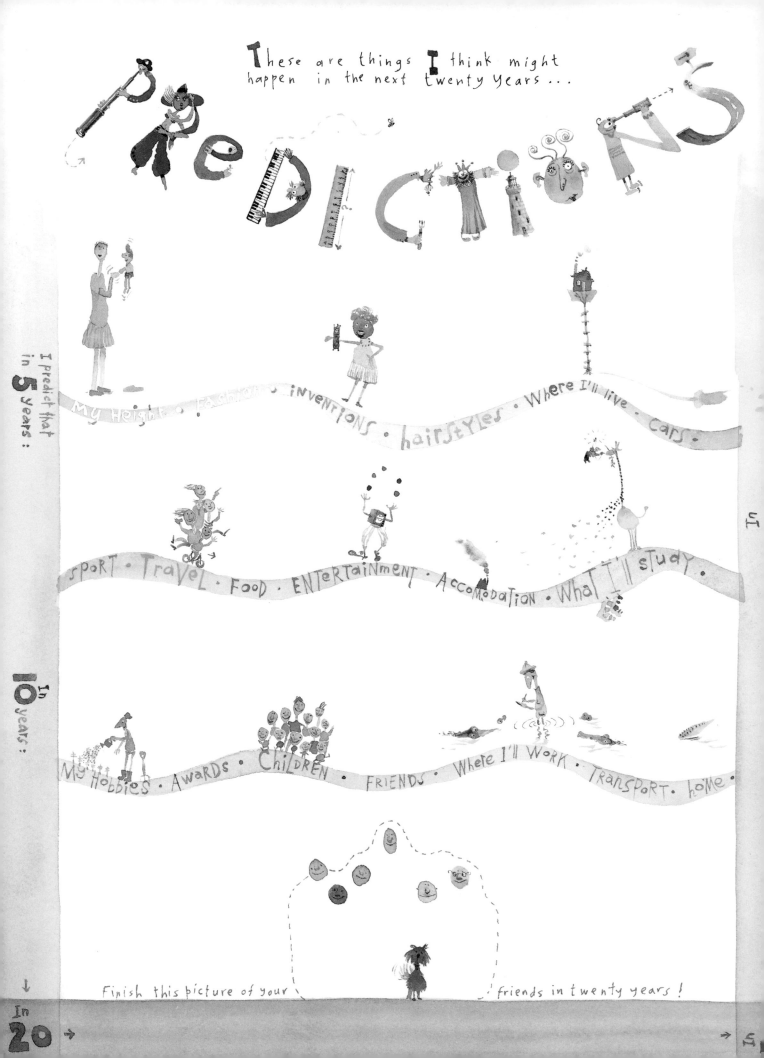

These are things I think might happen in the next twenty years...

PREDICTIONS

My Height · Fashion · Inventions · hairstyles · Where I'll live · cars ·

sport · Travel · Food · ENTERTAINMENT · Accommodation · What I'll study ·

My Hobbies · Awards · Children · FRIENDS · Where I'll Work · Transport · home ·

I predict that in 5 years :

In 10 years :

In 20

Finish this picture of your friends in twenty years !

WHAT I MIGHT LOOK LIKE

picture of me as a teenager

My Pet

Me in front of my home

Me at 100 years old

Me, Now

A great moment in my life

A drawing of me and my family.

THE BOSS

CERTIFICATE

(almost) THE TRUTH and NOTHING BUT THE TRUTH

THIS is to CERTIFY THAT ALL of the INFORMATION in THIS BOOK is the TRUTH

signed: _____

witnessed: _____

Suitable witnesses: policeman, teacher, doctor, parent, lollypop person.